# EARTH ANGELS

A True Story of Heroism in the Face of Tragedy

*Joey Lynn Sarkees*

iUniverse, Inc.

New York   Bloomington

Earth Angels
A True Story of Heroism in the Face of Tragedy

iUniverse books may be ordered through booksellers or by contacting:

iUniverse
1663 Liberty Drive
Bloomington, IN 47403
www.iuniverse.com
1-800-Authors (1-800-288-4677)

Because of the dynamic nature of the Internet, any Web addresses or
links contained in this book may have changed since publication and
may no longer be valid. The views expressed in this work are solely those
of the author and do not necessarily reflect the views of the publisher,
and the publisher hereby disclaims any responsibility for them.

ISBN: 978-1-4502-0534-4 (pbk)
ISBN: 978-1-4502-0536-8 (cloth)
ISBN: 978-1-4502-0535-1 (ebk)

Library of Congress Control Number: 2010905399

Printed in the United States of America

iUniverse rev. date: 5/18/2010

For Martin

## Indiana University of Pennsylvania Women's Rugby Club Pregame Cheer

I am a winner.

I feel great.

I am special.

Today is the greatest day of my life.

Everyday I am getting better and better.

I am focused.

I am determined.

I will not be denied.

I speak no negatives.

I have no fears.

I will do whatever it takes because I am a team player.

I am an important part of this unified team.

1-2-3 Scooters!

# Acknowledgments

To the Earth Angels—Molly Perchinski, Crystal Brenning, Chrissy May, Karen Reidel, Joeylyn Miller, Kristen Double, Jenna Sloan, Jessica Sheetz, Justine Metzger, Erin Harkins, Steph DeHaven, Amanda Cobb, Lauren Culley, Ariel Baum, Audra Turner, Rachel Stern, and Jamie Noble—thank you for sharing your stories of bravery, tragedy, and teamwork; thank you for promptly answering countless e-mails and telephone calls; and thank you for digging deep to remember even the smallest of details. You are seventeen of the bravest women I have ever met, and I consider it a privilege to be able to share your story. To honor your accomplishments, 20 percent of the royalties generated by sales of *Earth Angels* will be donated to a foundation created to help foster and promote women's athletics.

Thank you to the following individuals for their assistance: Terry Appolonia, Dr. Lawrence Pettit, Joseph Brimmeier, Carl DeFebo Jr., Jeff Beard, Scott Shaffer, Julie Foudy, Dr. Larry Bouma, and Bud and Jackie Perchinski.

Thank you to the following organizations for their assistance: Indiana University of Pennsylvania (IUP), IUP

Women's Rugby Club who so kindly allowed me to practice with them during one of my visits, IUP's Student Co-op, the Pennsylvania Turnpike Commission, Women's Sports Foundation, *Reader's Digest*, the Pennsylvania State Police, and the families of the Earth Angels for providing newspaper clippings and hosting interviews.

A lot of intimate details about the victims of April 5, 2003, were shared by their loved ones. Words can't express how grateful I am to these family members for allowing me to share their stories. I hope the relationships we have created are ones that last for many years to come. Thank you for everything.

Thank you to my family for short-notice babysitting, excellent editing, and lots of encouragement.

Most important, thank you to my husband, Martin, for reminding me regularly that I was meant for this. Here's to being eighty and eating ice cream.

To my boys, you are by far my greatest accomplishments.

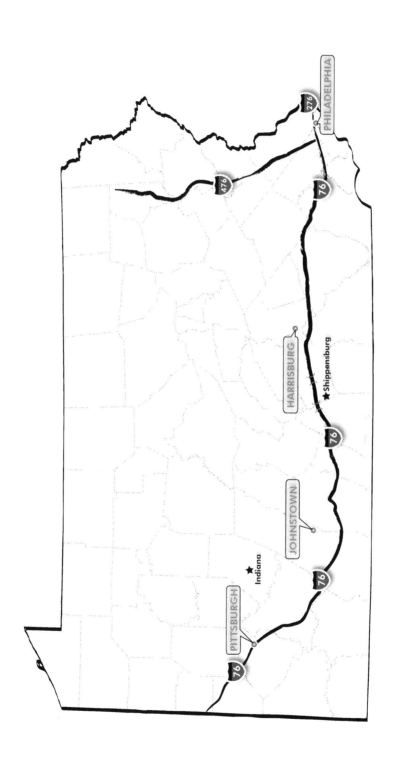

# Contents

# Introduction

At its essence, *Earth Angels* focuses on social evolution and a strong sense of empowerment by a group of young female athletes who clearly displayed a sense of strength that was generated from the bond they formed playing a team sport together. These brave young women who ran into danger while so many others were running out and spent hours working as one unit to help the helpless, learned a lot of the tactics they used from playing sports. Their ability to communicate without talking, rely on each other, and make quick decisions were all rugby skills that they used on the pitch.

The idea to write *Earth Angels* wasn't exactly mine. After numerous trips on the Pennsylvania Turnpike and long discussions about what it must have been like for seventeen young female college rugby players to save countless lives while amid one of the worst accidents in Pennsylvania

Turnpike history, my husband Martin proposed that I write their story.

Both longtime athletes and competitive rugby players, we were floored at the bravery, selflessness, and impeccable courage that members of the Indiana University of Pennsylvania Women's Rugby Club displayed. With a personal tie to the club, a degree in journalism and experience writing about rugby, I saw *Earth Angels* as the opportunity to share the story of a group of noble young women who saved countless lives so selflessly. I also saw it as an opportunity to promote women's sports and expose the positive effects that female athletics can have on a young woman.

I was introduced to the sport of rugby for the first time during my sophomore year at IUP in 1996. I distinctly remember standing on the sidelines while watching the IUP men play and contemplating exactly how I could find fifteen brave souls who were willing to play a collision sport. Fortunately, I joined forces with a group of brave pioneers whose objective was the same as mine: recreate the IUP Women's Rugby Club. The club had existed in the past but had folded for various reasons in the late eighties. A few months after, with the help of longtime men's coach Dr. Larry Bouma and some of his players, two dedicated coaches, and a group of women of all sizes, shapes, and backgrounds, the IUP Scooters were created.

I have found a lot of comfort in the fact that the diversity of the club, the purpose, and the strong bond among teammates have not changed through the years. While researching, I learned that so much today remains as it did back then, as it also did during the Earth Angels tenure. This includes the location of the women's rugby house that is referred to in this book and the pure dedication and hard drive that make up the personalities of the team. The women still continue to make their own executive decisions and raise their own funds while continually increasing their level of play. They still present a united front, both on and off the rugby pitch, and still play a style of rugby that has earned them the respect of all of their opponents.

When people ask me why I still play rugby at age thirty-two, I tell them because it hasn't stopped being fun yet. Rugby is a combination of every sport I ever loved and a permanent part of my life. It is the reason I met my husband, a strong bond we share, and where we take our children on beautiful fall Saturday afternoons and cool spring mornings. It has allowed me to travel to places I never thought I would see and meet people from all walks of life who have become longtime friends. It has allowed me to become a member of an elite club of fine female athletes who aren't afraid to take a hit or get a little dirt under their nails. I play because after a long day at work, when I am tired and want nothing more than to lay down, rugby brings me back to life.

My rugby experience allowed me to relate to the teamwork and mental toughness that carried the IUP women through unforgettable hours of tragedy. My writing experience allowed me to tell their story of bravery and teamwork.

*Earth Angels* is a combination of my love of writing and rugby.

Dramatis Personae

| | |
|---|---|
| Chrissy May | Co-captain |
| Amanda Cobb | Co-captain |
| Jamie Noble | |
| Karen Reidel | |
| Lauren Culley | |
| Joeylyn Miller | |
| Jenna Sloan | |
| Kristen Double | |
| Crystal Brenning | Club president |
| Molly Perchinski | |
| Audra Turner | |
| Erin Harkins | |
| Stephanie DeHaven | |
| Justine Metzger | |
| Ariel Baum | |
| Rachel Stern | |
| Jessica Sheetz | |
| David Moyer | |
| Olivia Moyer | Fatality #1 |

| | |
|---|---|
| Isabella Moyer | Fatality #2 |
| Noah Moyer | Fatality #3 |
| Kim Atkins | Olivia's older sister |
| Anna Coventry | Olivia's older sister |
| Joseph Francis | Olivia's father |
| Caroline Darlington | Olivia's aunt |
| Richard Sampson | Fatality #4 |

IUP Representatives

| | |
|---|---|
| Dr. Lawrence K. Pettit | IUP President (1992-2003) |
| Terry Appolonia | IUP Director of the Center for Student Life |
| Dr. Anthony Joseph | Faculty advisor for the club |

Emergency Services

| | |
|---|---|
| Scott Shaffer | Captain of the Breezewood Fire Department |

Pennsylvania Turnpike Commission

| | |
|---|---|
| Joseph Brimmeier | CEO, Pennsylvania Turnpike Commission |
| Carl DeFebo, Jr. | Media and Public Relations Manager, Pennsylvania Turnpike Commission |

*Earth Angels* is based on a true story. Some names have been changed.

# Chapter One
# A Fog Rolls In

The burning vehicles from the initial accident and cars driving too fast for the horrendous fog conditions led to an eighteen-vehicle pileup. There were no escape routes for the cars. The sounds of metal slamming into metal and screeching brakes must have been gut-wrenching for everyone involved. Smoke continued to clog the air. Multiple cars were struck multiple times, and many lay still, blocking both lanes in various places on the Pennsylvania Turnpike.

Just when everyone thought the conditions couldn't get worse, two of the vehicles toward the tail end of the accident also caught fire. The fire quickly spread and ultimately damaged nine vehicles. Confusion and panic set in as drivers and passengers began to quickly exit their cars and hide behind the guardrails. The two separate fires in the eastbound lanes left many trapped, struggling to find protection.

The heavy fog continued to plague the turnpike as the six cars carrying the Indiana University of Pennsylvania women's rugby players continued eastbound. Visibility was at a minimum, and even headlights couldn't improve the conditions. A few of the drivers became concerned. The women began to wonder if the fog would make them late for their match. Moments later, getting to the match on time became the least of their concerns.

*     *     *

Saturday, April 5, 2003, began like every other game day for the Indiana University of Pennsylvania Women's Rugby Club. As usual, the women met at the rugby house early in the morning and immediately started their pregame rituals. The rookies began packing the cars with rugby balls, first-aid kits, water, uniforms, cleats, extra socks and shorts, ball pumps, and rugby bags. Some of the veterans declared themselves to be on french-braiding duty and worked on braiding their teammates' hair. Procrastinators molded their mouth guards in the kitchen, and a few of the women taped ankles, knees, and hands for injuries that resulted from previous rugby matches. Like normal college students, some were always hungry and walked to the deli next door to get breakfast or snacks for the lengthy car ride. The women were preparing for their match individually and as a team. They anticipated a long day because of the drive and because both a-side and b-side had matches.

Kickoff against Shippensburg University Women's Rugby Club was scheduled for 1:00 PM. The women predicted that the drive would take them nearly three hours. As for every away match, the women left together in six cars, following each other and staying in contact via cell phones.

As the caravan left Indiana, the women played music, called each other, and made predictions about the post-match team social. The social was an after-match party that was typically held at the home team's rugby house and was something to which the women looked forward. It was a chance for the home team to thank their opposition with food and drinks for traveling to them. The players put aside any tension that may have built up during the match and the outcome, as they toasted each other and sang traditional rugby songs. For those who weren't accustomed to the rugby way of life, the concept of the social was challenging. The main question was how could women who had spent the last eighty minutes tackling each other have a polite, friendly conversation afterward?

A little over an hour into the trip, one of the women had to use the bathroom. As the message was relayed, one car opted not to stop; Erin Harkins and Justine Metzger continued on. The rest of the women pulled into a gas station near an entrance onto the Pennsylvania Turnpike.

When the women were finished using the ladies' room and everyone was accounted for, the caravan started across the parking lot. Suddenly, the cars stopped. Molly Perchinski jumped out of Kristen Double's car to retrieve her wallet, which she had forgotten in the ladies' room. The women ended up blocking both the entrance and exit while they waited. Unhappy drivers began honking their horns at them while traffic lined up.

Eventually, Molly made her way back to Kristen's car, and the traffic jam cleared.

Again on their way, the women were content, expecting to play and win their match, socialize with their opponents, and continue to live the lives of carefree, innocent college students. It was Saturday; it was rugby day.

$*$ $*$ $*$

Valley-Hi Eagle Lake is a man-made lake located in Valley-Hi Borough, Pennsylvania. It covers almost forty acres and is privately owned. It's easy to speculate how the lake got its name, as it sits at the bottom of a valley, surrounded by numerous mountains that help compose the lengthy Appalachian mountain chain. The view of the lake is spectacular from the section of the Pennsylvania Turnpike that perches directly above it. Surrounded entirely by trees that line its banks, the lake is a welcomed, majestic escape for the eyes because of its earth-colored water, which breaks up the sea of trees.

Mile marker 166 of the Pennsylvania Turnpike sits high above the lake. This section of the interstate is just as beautiful and isolated as the lake itself. The accommodating highway carefully traverses an area that, from the road, appears unpopulated and isolated, filled only with trees and surrounded by mountains. This section of the interstate provides solitude to drivers with its scenic views of valleys below and mountains above.

Some of the fog that plagues this portion of the turnpike could potentially be linked to the location of Valley-Hi Eagle Lake.

*        *        *

It was foggy and damp that morning on the Pennsylvania Turnpike. The temperature was 55 degrees. David Moyer was driving east in the right lane. His wife was sitting in the passenger seat, and their children, eight-year-old Isabella and two-year-old Noah, were in the backseat. While approaching mile marker 166, the family encountered the dense fog. David slowed to a speed of forty miles per hour and cautiously turned on his hazards.

Behind him, Dylan Jenkins was driving his car at sixty miles per hour. According to the state police accident report, Jenkins' speed was too fast for the roadway and weather conditions. When David slowed down, Jenkins attempted to move into the left lane to avoid sideswiping the Moyers' vehicle. However, the front end of Jenkins' car hit the rear of the Moyers' car. Jenkins continued to steer to the left and began braking. He lost control of his vehicle and rotated counterclockwise while still applying his brakes. He slid for an unknown distance, eventually stopping, his car facing north and partially in the left-hand eastbound lane and partially on the median. He drove down the median into oncoming traffic and spent the next few minutes flashing his lights, warning cars to slow down because of the fog and the accident ahead.

Moyer continued in the right lane. He was trying to get to the shoulder when he was struck from behind by a tractor trailer driven by Andrew Dayton. According to the state police report, Dayton was also traveling too fast for the roadway and weather conditions at sixty-three miles per hour. The collision forced the Moyers' vehicle to the right, where it struck the guardrail. The car then rolled onto its passenger side and began rotating. The tractor trailer came to a stop partially in the right lane and partially on the shoulder. The Moyers' car came to rest with its passenger side lodged between the guardrail and the tractor trailer's axles. At some point during the collision, both vehicles caught fire.

The trapped family must have felt the heat coming from the back of their burning car immediately. With help from the driver of the tractor trailer, David was able to escape the inferno by way of the driver's side window. He attempted to save his family, but the vehicles were overcome by fire. He couldn't get them out. Moyer suffered severe burns and was taken by Hustontown EMS to Fulton County Medical Center. He was then flown to West Penn Burn Center in Pittsburgh, where he spent the next few days.

\*     \*     \*

The vehicles involved in the initial accident burning on the roadway and cars traveling at speeds too fast in the dense fog led to a second pileup, this one with eighteen vehicles, in the eastbound lanes that resulted in the death of fifty-five-year-old Richard Sampson. According to the state police report, Sampson was also traveling too fast for the roadway conditions. Failing to observe that traffic was almost completely stopped, Sampson struck the car in front of him. He was then struck from behind by another car. A fire quickly started in the two cars. Sampson was stuck in his car and burned to death.

With the fog still so thick that victims couldn't see anything until they were on top of it, a third accident occurred behind the first two in the eastbound lanes. This one involved two cars. Moments later, two more accidents occurred in the fog-plagued westbound lane of the interstate.

As a result, there were no escape routes for the cars.

\*     \*     \*

Erin Harkins and Justine Metzger were in the midst of all the chaos. As they proceeded eastbound on the turnpike, the fog continued to worsen. Eventually, it forced them to significantly reduce their speed. Harkins began to focus on the taillights of the vehicle in front of her because visibility had become severely limited. As they slowed, the women saw a vehicle on fire in front of them.

Harkins slammed on her brakes and barely avoided a collision with the car in front of her. Unfortunately, she was rear-ended by the car behind her. As the cars around them began to pile up, Harkins pulled her car onto the median to avoid being struck again. The women got out of the car and ducked between the guardrail and the median to avoid flying debris. Protecting their heads with their hands, they listened to screeching tires quickly followed by a loud crash. Realizing they were not out of harm's way, the women opted to follow another crash victim past the pileup, around burning vehicles, and through thorn bushes to safety on a grassy knoll on the side of the road. They took refuge under a billboard with other victims, some of whom were injured and disoriented, as they waited for the chaos to subside and help to arrive.

# Chapter Two
## Rugby as a Way of Life

Molly Perchinski is smart, beautiful, and kind. Her curly, brownish-red hair and sparkling blue eyes make her a natural beauty who turns heads as she enters a room. Tall and thin, Molly carries a confidence, both in her voice and stance that rarely exists even in top corporate executives. But when she cracks a smile, her face lights up, and the rest of her unique personality begins to filter out as she talks. It is easy to comprehend from the stories she shares about her family, college, her time as team captain for her rugby team, and the horrific event that changed her life that Molly has lived a lot in her short number of years.

Molly and her older sister and best friend, Sarah, were raised by their parents, Bud and Jackie. Molly's eyes light up as she describes her parents' supportive and thoughtful ways. She shared the story of a book of life lessons that they created for her when she turned twenty-one. They had called on family and friends to offer their words of wisdom to Molly and put all of them in a book for her. Her parents also supported decisions she made, such as the decision to play rugby.

The environment in their home was a loving one in which the girls were encouraged to be strong-willed individuals but also kind and thoughtful. They were bred on confidence and high moral standards and were encouraged to always share their feelings.

Unlike many other parents, the Perchinskis knew they couldn't change certain characteristics about their daughter, such as her fearlessness. According to Jackie, Molly was the kind of kid who had no fear. She was the one they worried would dive down a flight of stairs or jump in a pool in the middle of March. Although Molly did succeed in participating in some very scary events, she also continued to push the envelope without ever feeling real fear.

This fearlessness stayed with Molly through her teenage years and into college. In 2001 Molly began attending Indiana University of Pennsylvania (IUP) in Indiana, Pennsylvania. She enrolled in IUP's art program with the intention of quickly transferring to a different college.

However, that never happened. As Molly grew comfortable at IUP, she began to explore the options of playing a sport. Perhaps it was because of her innate fearlessness that the ex-swimmer sought a sport that offered good competition and an element of risk. Much to her pleasure, Molly found what she was looking for in the IUP Women's Rugby Club.

"I distinctly remember standing in the university library staring at a flyer advertising women's rugby. I remember thinking that there actually were people like me who had a fierce athletic drive and weren't afraid to take a hit," said Molly, who was a sophomore at the time. "When I first joined the team, I never thought I would find my other sisters." But before long, Molly knew she had found her niche.

Like with everything else, Molly bolted full-speed into rugby. "We went to Division I during my rookie semester, and the team had no one to play second row. I was thrown in and ran around the field on pure adrenaline rather than understanding the game." Desperate to understand and improve her play for a game she was quickly coming to love, Molly dedicated all of her time to rugby. Her actions paid off, as she was voted "Rookie of the Year" later that season.

Molly loved the game, but even more, she loved her teammates. She loved the camaraderie that came from working together toward a common goal. She loved going to practice and spending entire Saturdays and the rest of their free time together. She loved team dinners, team socials, and the depth of the bond they felt from sacrificing their bodies and defending each other on the pitch. She loved being a part of a structured, organized, and good rugby club.

Diversity is a large part of women's rugby and is something that exists among the players on every rugby team. The IUP women weren't any different. This was something that Molly loved. She took pride in the fact that her teammates had such varied life experiences; some of her teammates were sorority sisters, and others had begun playing rugby in high school. She enjoyed working with women from different backgrounds; they ranged from lifetime sportswomen to first-time athletes. They were all different heights, weights, and sizes, yet there was a place for each of them on the pitch. They all had their individual strengths, and they came together for the common goal of rugby. Regardless of their backgrounds, they unified to play a sport they loved for a team they loved. For Molly, this provided a sense of tremendous depth and passion.

The women were teammates and also very close friends. They bled together, sweated together, cried together, and celebrated together. "I loved that not many people were cut out for rugby, and I was part of the team of women that were. I loved being inspired by the passion of the sport and inspiring others with that passion. I loved being able to feel a sense of accomplishment that we all did it together, as a team, without a coach, and were beyond capable of that responsibility," said Molly.

Molly also felt a lot of power and drive from being part of a women's athletic team. She knew that in being a female athlete, she was a clear representation of the social evolution of women in history. Not long ago, women weren't permitted to play sports, let alone join a team. Molly was part of a greater movement to promote women in sports. As an athlete, she had more opportunities and a greater impact on society.

"We were playing the same sport, running similar plays, and using the same equipment as the men's team. To me, that was very exciting. Usually, in most sports, there are differences between female and male versions, such as ball sizes and time of play. But rugby is gender-equal, and we played the game just like the guys," said Molly.

Intent on being the best second row on the team, Molly dedicated herself to rugby and her team. Determined to make a difference on and off the field, Molly easily rose through the ranks of the club by running for executive positions. She served as team social chair, which fit her easygoing personality. The position put her in charge of arranging social gatherings with other organizations on campus. She would go on to become president of the club, a time-consuming position that often involved making many difficult and important leadership decisions. The sport of rugby was growing quickly across the world, particularly for women, and Molly wanted to help promote the movement.

Serving as the team's president enabled her to fulfill this desire and was a whole new challenge for Molly for many reasons. For starters, the team did not have a dedicated coach. Although they did receive coaching assistance from the men's club from time to time, the women didn't have a designated coach who attended every practice or game. Thus, many challenging decisions and difficult conversations were held between the executive board and the team captains. Topics included where club money would be spent and the most effective way to travel. The women were responsible for their own internal system of checks and balances. As a result, Molly was partially responsible for pulling everything together both on and off the field. Although this may seem like an easy task, it was anything but simple. The club had to run smoothly, and she was responsible for that. Her role involved dealing with over thirty different personalities, submitting proposals for funds, contributing to making travel arrangements, and attending university meetings to plead for more funding.

Besides the unique bond she shared with her teammates as part of a growing sport, the most fulfilling experience for Molly was the opportunity and ability to pass on her love of the game to new players. Although a lot of time and energy was spent teaching rookies the basics of the game, different positions, and numerous plays, the team was rewarded in the end because they had the opportunity to watch what they had taught play out on the pitch. Even if the rookies took a little longer to comprehend the game, they made up for their lack of knowledge with their passion. According to Molly, the quote, "Rugby is not just a sport; it's a lifestyle," described her rugby career. That is also what she tried to pass on to new players who would continue to pass it on through the years.

"I was consumed and in love with everything the sport

had to offer," she said humbly. "The sport had a strategic competition, and my expectations went in progressive steps, continually trying to take on and challenge myself so I could continue to feel a sense of accomplishment."

On Saturday, April 5, 2003, she faced the greatest challenge of her life. And for the first time, Molly Perchinski felt real fear.

# Chapter Three
## Surprising Dad

Twenty-nine-year-old Olivia Moyer was so excited to visit her father in her native state of Connecticut that she didn't even tell him she was coming. She wanted to arrive at his house, knock on his door, and see the shock and excitement on his face as he opened it and found her standing there with her family. The plan sounded fitting for a woman whose family had nicknamed her "Smiles" because of her bubbly, cheerful nature.

"We had this whole plan to meet at my dad's house and surprise him," said Kim, Olivia's older sister. Kim and her family lived a very short driving distance from their father, Joseph, and their oldest sister, Anna. Visits between the family members were frequent, and Olivia's coming home was the icing on the cake for the tight-knit clan. "Olivia really didn't want him to know she was coming."

Olivia's husband, David, a sergeant in the United States Army, had saved his vacation time and earned a month-long leave. So, the Moyers packed Isabella and Noah into their 1996 Ford Explorer and left their home on Saint Francis army base in Idaho en route to Connecticut.

Olivia and David met during their middle school years. During their early years of high school, both their families moved, but that didn't stop David from pursuing Olivia. He took the opportunity to inquire about her when he bumped into one of her friends when Olivia was in eleventh grade. Soon after, they were reconnected and had been together ever since. After boot camp, David proposed to Olivia, and they prepared to begin their lives together. David was to be stationed in Germany, and Olivia was going with him.

"I guess he couldn't dream of living or moving on without her, so they got married and moved to Germany almost instantly," said Kim, who also kept in close touch with her sister. "They lived there for six years, and that's where Isabella was born."

As with most emotionally attached families, it was very difficult saying good-bye to the baby of four siblings and her new husband, whom the family also cared for deeply. It was Olivia's first move away from home, and everyone knew they would miss her loving, caring, good-natured personality.

Trips home were rare, but the Moyers made it work when they could. Their families were their priority, and the Moyers never lost sight of what was most important. When Olivia's mother, Sophia, was dying of cancer in 1998, Olivia and Isabella came home for months to help care for her. Olivia also became an important part of a network of support for her father. Unfortunately, she had to fly back to Germany two days after the funeral. Even then, she called her father every night to check in with him and talk.

It was also around that time that Olivia began collecting angels. For birthdays and holidays, her family would send her angels that she kept in a curio cabinet. Being surrounded by them made Olivia feel better and gave her a sense of comfort after her mother's death. There was one angel in particular that she adored. It was a gift from Anna. The figurine was of three angels holding hands. It was intended to symbolize the three sisters and their strong bond. Kim also sent Olivia an angel that played Bette Midler's "Wind Beneath My Wings." That song was one of their mother's favorites.

Often described as the glue that held everyone together, Olivia was also a dedicated, full-time mom. She loved her children deeply and passionately. This was proven in the time she spent volunteering with Isabella's Girl Scout troop as a way to spend more time with her only daughter. She also sent e-mails and pictures by the dozen of her beautiful, happy, healthy children. They were very much like her: full of life and fun loving. Although Noah was born in Connecticut when Olivia was home visiting, the family hadn't been able to spend a lot of time with him. They didn't really know him except for the stories that Olivia and David shared.

This trip home would be the fifth for Olivia and one that was to be full of many family events. Everyone was looking forward to seeing how much Isabella had grown and getting to know Noah. He was turning three in May, and a birthday party was planned for him. The family also planned a baby shower for Anna. Even their aunt Caroline and her husband would be making the trip north from South Carolina.

Extremely anxious and excited to see her baby sister, Anna had been tracking the Moyers' trip from Idaho to Connecticut on a map that her children had posted on their wall. Olivia would call Anna as the family traveled through various states, and Anna would point to the spot on the map. It helped the children understand how far their uncle, aunt, and cousins had traveled to see them and how close they were getting.

On April 5, 2003, Olivia called Anna to let her know that the family was still at their hotel. Everyone had showered, and they were preparing to leave the hotel, get breakfast, and get back on the road. Anna's response was, "Okay, drive safely and wear your seat belts." She also told her sister to make sure that David drove because the weather was bad that day.

# Chapter Four
## Game Day

On the morning of the accident, the IUP Women's Rugby Club left Indiana to begin their journey to a competitive rugby match. It was a typical Saturday, and they were expected at Shippensburg University for a 1:00 PM kickoff. The women were busy reflecting on Thursday afternoon's practice, strategizing about the match against Shippensburg, and discussing what they could expect from their opponent.

The team included Chrissy May, a sweet-faced twenty-one-year-old senior who played second row. May shared the captain responsibility with twenty-one-year-old junior fly-half, Amanda Cobb. As captains of a coach-less team, the women shared a lot of significant duties that only quality leaders could handle. They were responsible for organizing practice, keeping track of attendance at practice, and selecting the lineup for the game-day match. Fortunately for the team, both women possessed natural leadership and communication skills that made them highly effective.

The seniors who led the team in experience and knowledge were twenty-one-year-old Jamie Noble, a tough, long-standing member of the club who played hooker; twenty-two-year-old outside center Karen Reidel; and twenty-two-year-old Lauren Culley, who also played hooker. These three women were looked to time and time again by the younger rookie class because of their rugby wisdom and experience.

The juniors included Joeylyn Miller, a nineteen-year-old strong-shouldered wing forward who began playing rugby in high school; Jenna Sloan, a twenty-year-old who used her unusual speed to her advantage while playing wing; and inside centers Kristen Double and Crystal Brenning.

The team also had a large rookie class that season, which included twenty-year-old sophomore Audra Turner, who excelled at the position of scrumhalf; nineteen-year-old Erin Harkins, who played outside center; and nineteen-year-old freshman Steph DeHaven, who began playing prop in high school. Spunky ex-cheerleader Justine Metzger played the position of eight man. Twenty-one-year-old sophomore Ariel Baum played flanker and hooker. Eighteen-year-old freshman Rachel Stern played fly-half, and twenty-year-old Jessica Sheetz played center.

Although the IUP rugby team was full of diverse talent and experience, they shared several characteristics that caused them to bond in that special, nebulous way that most athletes strive for but rarely find. Though they were young, carefree, and innocent college athletes in their prime, the women had obstacles to overcome.

Although they were a recognized university club sport, the women received a set amount of financial support from the student co-op. As a result, they did all of their own fund-raising, wrote their own bylaws, and organized themselves. Their uniforms were old and worn, and they drove their own cars to matches and practices.

Shortly before the beginning of the Scooters' fall season in 2002, the highly competitive team voted and agreed to move to Division I rugby. Historically, Division I is for large colleges and universities with competitive, well-established rugby programs. Even as the Scooters made this difficult transition, the amount of support didn't increase.

"We moved to Division I because we wanted to play rugby at a higher level," said Jamie Noble, a seasoned veteran at the time of the change. "It would only make us a better team, and we knew that." Noble also pointed out that the club had also graduated several significant veterans the spring before, which made playing Division I more of a struggle.

"Playing Division I rugby made me feel like we were the 'Bad News Bears,'" said Molly. "We didn't have a coach and desperately needed new uniforms."

Their competition would often drive to games in team buses and would be wearing matching wind suits. "We were running our own team, managing all of our own funds, and managing ourselves while our opponents' coaches and trainers lined the fields."

The university supported a large number of clubs, and as a result, the women didn't receive as much financial assistance as they would have liked. From a competitive standpoint, they had the potential to be successful playing Division I; from a financial standpoint, they did not. Playing Division I required extensive traveling and extensive funding, two obstacles with which the club would continue to struggle. They were responsible for organizing and paying for travel arrangements, which included hotels, meals, transportation, and other incidental expenses. Almost all of the matches were played in the Midwest, easily a full-day drive from IUP. In addition, there were strict USA Rugby laws by which they needed to abide, which included paying annual union dues.

Although the women organized numerous fund-raisers, from car washes to T-shirt sales, during the year, the money was never enough.

They had no one but each other to rely on to push their sport and team forward. Almost all of them had been athletes prior to playing rugby, and all of them knew they wanted to do something in college. Rugby was their something, and they fought for it.

The spring 2003 season was proving to be a successful one, and the women were focused on playing smart rugby, being as physically fit as possible and staying positive. Prior to their match against Shippensburg, they were having a stellar season that consisted of demolishing their regular opponents. They had defeated regularly scheduled opponent Juniata College by a score of sixty to zero. The women also completely overpowered California University of Pennsylvania, also a regular opponent, by a score of thirty to zero.

In the rugby world, where one try is equal to five points and a conversion kick, which accompanies every try, is worth two points, these games were complete blowouts. The only real opposition that the women faced was at Cooper's Lake, an annual tournament held in Slippery Rock, Pennsylvania. Continuing with the powerful play, the women earned a spot in the championship match. Unfortunately, they were defeated.

The Scooters were anticipating a victorious end to the season with their upcoming match against Shippensburg. They were also looking forward to traveling to Eastern Pennsylvania for the West Chester University Women's Collegiate Classic Rugby Tournament.

# Chapter Five
# The Lord's Prayer

Karen Reidel and her passenger, Chrissy May, were slowly inching along behind a tractor trailer in the left-hand lane. They were in complete disbelief as to the density of the fog and helpless against it. Nothing they did was contributing to improving Reidel's visibility. Frustrated and nervous, the women contemplated calling their opponents to let them know the team would be late.

Through the dense fog, Reidel saw what looked like headlights flashing in the median, facing oncoming traffic. Realizing another driver was trying to communicate to oncoming traffic that there was trouble ahead, Reidel slammed on her brakes. Her car stopped mere inches from the now stationary tractor trailer the girls had been following. According to Reidel, had she not seen the flashing headlights, she would have slammed into the rear of the tractor trailer.

Kristen Double's experience was similar. With Molly in the passenger seat, Double slammed on her brakes to avoid striking the car in front of her. That car's windshield had shattered upon impact with the car in front of it.

Jamie Noble, along with passengers Steph DeHaven, Ariel Baum, and Lauren Culley, was driving the last team car. Although she was trying to keep a safe distance from the car in front of her because of the hazardous conditions, Noble was also forced to brake quickly. Because the women traveled on the turnpike frequently, they knew the decline in speed indicated a problem ahead. They began to wonder what had happened and wasted no time in finding out.

As the women waited in their stationary cars, in complete whiteout conditions, they began to hear popping sounds and then explosions. The smell of something burning, which some of the women described as smelling like baked potatoes, consumed the air as accident victims began screaming for help. The women would later learn that a tractor trailer that was burning was hauling potatoes. Because it had caught fire, the potatoes were burning too. The sound of potatoes exploding would last for hours until the tractor trailer was removed from the scene.

Even then, the women were unaware of the severity of the situation and their primary worry was still being late for their match; they began to get out of their cars and gather on the side of the road. They took roll to make sure their teammates were there. Realizing that Erin Harkins' car was unaccounted for, the women immediately became concerned. Their fears were eased when Harkins and Metzger called to say they were extremely frightened but unharmed.

At this point, the seriousness of what was happening around them began to set in. Panic struck the women as they stood huddled in the densest fog any of them had ever seen, still unable to see even inches in front of them. Still surrounded by explosions, the smell of burning potatoes and vehicles, and screams, the women wondered exactly what was happening. It was clear their cars weren't moving.

A natural leader, Chrissy May began walking eastbound on the turnpike into the fog, toward the black smoke to find out what was delaying the women's trip and what exactly was burning. While she was walking, the fog lifted just enough for her to see that there was a horrific accident surrounding the team.

"I could hear people talking as I was walking, and I could hear crying. I couldn't see anything, but I could hear explosions every so often," said May. "The fog opened up a little bit, and I saw people everywhere. I could see bodies everywhere, and I could see that many of the cars had hit each other. I remember thinking we had to help these people. I couldn't tell how many people were hurt, but I knew we needed to do something."

Overwhelmed and unsure as to how many people were injured, May was quick to relay what she saw to her nervous but eager teammates. Based on May's observations and the smells and sounds around them, the women realized that the accidents that had occurred were extremely serious.

"I still can't explain the feeling," said May. "I saw what was happening and knew we had to do something right away."

The women also recognized that there weren't enough, if any, emergency service workers on the scene to help all of the injured victims. Without hesitation, the women immediately made the most heroic decision of their young lives: they chose to help.

"So many people didn't get out of their cars to help victims. It was just so natural for us to help," said May. "I never understood it. You would think that people would go help people."

A man running past the women spotted them standing on the side of the road. He quickly asked if any of them were CPR or first-aid certified and if they could help any of the victims. Fortunately, at least eight of the women were certified. They responded that they would help, and the man passed them a box full of medical supplies. He told them to help whomever they could. To this day, the women don't know where the supplies came from because emergency service workers had not arrived yet.

"When everyone saw the accident, everyone went in their own direction," said May, reflecting on who they helped first. "I remember seeing my teammates, and everyone was helping someone."

Molly quickly went to work with Audra Turner and Chrissy. They spotted an elderly man who was sitting with his wife, covered in blood. He was positioned on his knees with her head in his lap. Unable to locate the source of the blood, the women quickly realized the man had been burned and both he and his wife were in shock. Turner began cutting the man's pants as Molly comforted his wife. The couple informed the women that they had been traveling with their granddaughter and they believed she had been thrown from the car. Molly and Chrissy began to search frantically for the young girl, whom they located in the woods nearby.

"The granddaughter was lying on a backboard on the edge of the woods," said May, who remembers comforting the fear-stricken girl.

After reuniting her with her grandmother, a relieved Molly also continued to comfort the family. In a positive attempt to distract the young girl, Molly asked her if she played any sports.

"I was asking questions, and she told me she played basketball," said Molly. "I was trying to really comfort them and let them know everything was going to be okay."

Amanda Cobb joined a group of girls who were helping an elderly couple who had sat in their car for nearly two hours after the accident, in shock. The man was still tightly gripping the steering wheel; the windshield had been shattered after they rear-ended a tractor trailer. The couple was on their way to visit their grandchildren and had Easter baskets in the backseat. The windshield was indented as a result of the impact, and broken glass had fallen on their laps. The glass that was still connected to the windshield was pointing inward, making it difficult to retrieve them from the car. Panicked and suffering from shock, the couple thought they may also have been suffering from broken bones.

"Our concern was that it wasn't a good idea to have them behind a tractor trailer that could blow up," said Cobb. "We didn't know if we should move them, but we ended up pulling the seat backward and unclipping both of the seat belts."

Soon after, emergency crews arrived with backboards to transport the victims. The women continued to hold the couple's hands and calm them until they were safe.

Through the smoke, fire, and confusion, there were moments so surreal they seemed to be taken out of a book. As Amanda Cobb was searching the roadway and looking for more victims to help, she noticed an elderly woman still in a car in the middle of a heap of metal and debris. The woman appeared dazed and disoriented and asked Cobb for help. Cobb escorted the woman away from the burning vehicles and onto the bank above the roadway; the woman remained confused. Cobb didn't notice that the woman's head was bleeding until she sat her down.

"I put something on her face," said Cobb. "She was looking around and asking for her husband. Then she told me she needed her glasses and that they were still in the car."

Nervous about leaving the woman alone for too long, Cobb quickly dashed to her car and found the glasses. When she came back, the woman said, "I want to see the face of the angel who saved my life." This emotional, yet terrifying, story was one that Cobb shared with her teammates and family.

The medics soon arrived and put the injured woman on a stretcher. Through it all, Cobb held her hand and reassured the woman, along with herself, that everything was going to be okay.

As the afternoon progressed, the rugby team never grew tired of helping, but they always felt like there were never enough of them to help everyone. Still working in small groups and helping who and where they could, the women continued providing aid. They were instructed by emergency workers to check every vehicle and make sure all victims had been helped.

Beyond providing their comforting presence, they transported wounded victims on stretchers to ambulances, helped apply oxygen masks, distributed Band-Aids and wraps to victims, stopped bleeding by applying pressure, and ran side by side with paramedics, waiting for directions.

Obviously in moving quickly from one victim to the next, the women never stopped to think about themselves. After hours of running through knee-high thick brush, Chrissy May's legs were scraped and cut. However, she refused to tend to them or her shoeless foot because she knew that the victims needed her more.

"I didn't want to stop to do anything for myself," said a humble May. "There were so many people that needed help, and we all just kept moving."

The women also offered their personal items, such as phones, to the victims. Kristen Double recalled one man who placed a call to locate his son. The two men had been traveling together but in separate cars. Initially panic-stricken with the thought that his son was involved in the accident, the man was relieved to learn that he had passed through the fog prior to the accident. Steph DeHaven gave a woman a pair of extra pants, and a number of the teammates gave their shoes to victims.

As the women continued to do whatever it took to help, they weren't able to ignore the fact that their situation was life threatening. Almost all of them had seen what little remained of the Moyer family's Explorer, and it was a clear indication of how dangerous the accident scene still was. The vehicle remained lodged between the guardrail and the tractor trailer axles. By this time, it was almost unrecognizable. The area around it was littered with stuffed animals, toys, and kids' suitcases. The Explorer was completely burned. The three victims, Olivia, Isabella, and Noah, were still inside.

"Emergency workers eventually put white sheets over the car," said Molly. "It was one of those situations where they told you not to look, but you still looked. I can't imagine not only losing your wife and children but seeing them and not being able to get them out."

For Jamie Noble, it was an image she will never forget. "I always believed that car seats were supposed to protect you, but not in this case. The thing that I remember the most is seeing the kids still stuck in their car seats and hearing people screaming."

Even as fire department and medical personnel arrived, the women's efforts to help continued. According to the state police reports, six fire companies and EMS units responded to the accident. They included Breezewood, Everett, Bedford, Six Mile Run, Hustontown, and McConnellsburg. In addition, Raystown, Bedford, Shawnee Valley, Six Mile Run, Hustontown, and McConnellsburg all provided EMS units. The physical location and severity of the accident made the journey to the scene extremely difficult and time-consuming for emergency services. With both lanes of the turnpike gridlocked and shut down, many of the emergency vehicles had to find alternate routes. Numerous fire engines and ambulances traveled on the shoulders of the turnpike, if they could get around the cars that were littering the highway. Desperate to help, Everett Fire Company traveled down Route 30, a road which parallels that section of the turnpike. They entered a business parking lot and cut the turnpike's right-of-way fence to gain access.

The women assisted emergency service workers by helping them take down the fence. They also carried the medical equipment from victim to victim, allowing the EMTs to get to everyone faster. They received support and guidance from emergency service workers who were outnumbered by the injured.

The heaps of metal that were once cars also prevented fire engines and ambulances from gaining access to victims on the opposite side of the turnpike. Scott Shaffer was the captain of the Breezewood Fire Department at the time of the accident. "We called Hustontown Fire Department to come in from the west in the eastbound lane, because we couldn't get access through the wreckage to get to the eastbound lane. I have been in fire service for sixteen years, but this was the worst multiple casualties accident I have seen," said Shaffer. He went on to say that the accident was one that remained with him for years. "Just the magnitude of that many victims and fatalities, you expect the worst, but it was worse than you expected."

The decision to implement Plan X, which means all traffic is diverted off of the turnpike at designated interchanges, came quickly after the accident. All eastbound traffic was detoured off of the turnpike at the Breezewood interchange, and all westbound traffic was stopped at the Carlisle interchange on the east side.

In the end, the fog contributed to four deaths: twenty-nine-year-old Olivia Moyer, eight-year-old Isabella Moyer, two-year-old Noah Moyer, and fifty-five-year-old Richard Sampson. All of the victims burned to death in their vehicles.

An additional twenty-five people were injured, some critically. The devastating fog resulted in five accidents between both the eastbound and westbound lanes. Over twenty-five vehicles, many of which were burned so severely that the state police couldn't read their identification numbers, were involved in the accident. Cranes and large machinery were brought in to remove some vehicles from the roadway. The Pennsylvania Turnpike was closed for nearly twelve hours. The number of lives saved by the IUP Women's Rugby Club was countless.

It is unclear how long the women's rugby team stayed at the crash site. Naturally, their match was no longer their priority. They helped clear debris from the road and continued to assist victims. When it seemed that their selfless task was complete, they gathered together on the side of the turnpike, exhausted, hungry, thirsty, and emotional. After everything they had witnessed, the women joined hands and recited the Lord's Prayer.

Photo courtesy of the Pennsylvania State Police

Photo courtesy of the Pennsylvania State Police

Photo courtesy of the Pennsylvania State Police

Photo courtesy of the Pennsylvania State Police

Photo courtesy of the Pennsylvania State Police

Photo courtesy of the Pennsylvania State Police

# Chapter Six
## Heroes of the Year

At 9:56 PM the next day, Bud Perchinski sent an e-mail to IUP president, Dr. Lawrence K. Pettit. His subject read: "Girls' Rugby Team." In his e-mail, Perchinski told a shortened version of what his daughter and her teammates had experienced the day before. He asked Pettit to praise the students and to thank them for their heart-warming contribution. This communication could possibly have been the first that the university had heard of the accident.

As expected, the university was quick to respond. On Monday, April 7, the women received a letter from Dr. Pettit addressed to their faculty advisor, Dr. Anthony Joseph. In it, Pettit expressed pride and gratitude to the women for their actions on the turnpike. Through his choice of compassionate words, it was clear that Pettit had an understanding as to what the women had witnessed at the top of the mountain. But he couldn't have expressed his empathy any better than he did in the last paragraph: "Please understand, though, that what you did on that mountain was something few others could have done." That sentence was repeated numerous times in the following months.

Initially, the women shared their stories with their families and close friends. However, word of their heroic actions and the countless lives they saved spread quickly throughout the university community. No detail of the day's events and the women's lifesaving actions was overlooked by the media and university officials. Students on campus talked at length about the danger the women placed themselves in and how brave they were for risking their own lives. Stories of burning vehicles littering the road and bleeding victims waiting for first aid became topics of conversation in the university cafeteria and women's rugby house. The weight of the women's selflessness was clear in the acknowledgments that they received.

IUP director of the Center for Student Life, Terry Appolonia, was also quick to respond to the news of their heroics. He too composed a letter to club president Crystal Brenning on April 7 in which he expressed his pride and gratitude for the actions of the IUP Women's Rugby Club. From the information he had compiled regarding the accident, Appolonia, like Pettit, came to understand the magnitude of the events and the actions taken by the women. He wasted no time in asking Brenning for the names and addresses of the rugby players who were present on that foggy morning. Like many to come, he wanted to personally recognize and thank each and every one of them.

"I was among the first to learn of the incident and initially was concerned for the well-being of our students," said Appolonia. "As I met with members of the team early the following week, I was truly astonished at the bravery and fortitude displayed by these women. To have been prepared to physically and emotionally respond so successfully to such a challenge is truly incredible."

IUP's Office of Media Relations distributed a press release to a number of media outlets the same day, including the Associated Press. Again, the women received extensive praise and accolades for their actions. They were also once again recognized by Pettit, who is quoted as saying, "I am particularly proud of these students for their heroic efforts, risking injury to themselves to assist the crash victims." Pettit also sent a letter of recognition to Brenning.

Wanting to hear the tragic details of the accident, Appolonia then requested to meet with Brenning. He also extended an invitation for Brenning, along with Dr. Joseph, to attend the university's annual Service-Learning Recognition Banquet being held that week. Hosted by Dr. Pettit, the banquet recognizes students who have excelled in service to the campus and community, and faculty members who assisted them in doing so.

Seven days later, each IUP rugby player who had been

present at the crash site also received a letter of recognition from Appolonia. As in his previous letter, Appolonia expressed his gratitude and pride in the women. He recognized that the women's actions were lifesaving, and he seemed to comprehend the extensive amount of time the women spent on the turnpike after the accident offering aid. It was clear by the number of head faculty members copied on the letter that the women and their actions were making a tremendous impact on the university. They were also quick to reach out and offer counseling services.

The university wasn't the only organization to express support and gratitude to the women. In the days following what is considered one of the worst accidents in Pennsylvania Turnpike history, the IUP Women's Rugby Club received an enormous amount of unsought media attention. Chrissy May recalled the first time a news crew requested an interview.

According to May, she was returning to the women's rugby house from class when she saw a news van parked outside. As she entered the house, the news team asked for permission to interview her. As other residents of the rugby house came home, the news team continued interviewing the women in their living room. Numerous local television stations in the Pittsburgh area also aired the story.

The newspaper coverage that the women received was also astonishing. Numerous hometown newspapers were quick to claim the women as their own. Many of them printed features about individual players or the team. They all followed one theme: pride and amazement that a group of young college female athletes had committed such a selfless act. There were some players, like Molly, who saved everything. As part of the healing process, Molly created a scrapbook that was over twenty pages long, filled with colorful paper, quotes, and stickers. The scrapbook includes local and Pittsburgh area newspaper articles as well as an e-mail from *Reader's Digest* detailing the women's trip to New York City. Molly also included an article that was published in *IUP Magazine* as a sports feature, which again glorified the women's actions, as well as articles from *The Penn*, IUP's newspaper.

The following September, the women once again were honored by the university when they received a Resolution of Appreciation. Along with their families, they were invited to numerous events throughout the day to celebrate IUP Family Day. They were each awarded medals by the university for being exemplary citizens and were also invited to attend the IUP football game, where they were recognized during halftime.

The women also received support from the university staff, including one employee from the mathematics department who enclosed a donation with a letter. His message was clear as he wrote, "You showed the best of IUP that day, and there are many people who will never forget what you did for them."

*       *       *

The Outstanding Citizenship Award is a prestigious award that is presented to individuals and organizations that have assisted the Pennsylvania State Police in providing a significant service to the commonwealth. It is the highest award a Pennsylvania civilian can receive, and there are very few recipients in a given year. To be nominated for the award, a person's actions must have posed a substantial risk of serious injury or loss of life to him or her. The recipients must be nominated by a state police trooper. The nominations are reviewed and approved by the commissioner's review board, along with the commissioner.

On July 15, 2003, a letter from Captain David Points, the commanding officer of Troop T, the troop that specifically patrols the Pennsylvania Turnpike, was sent to each of the seventeen rugby players who were at the accident site. Impressed and moved by their actions, Points recognized that the women's assistance both saved lives and brought comfort to victims. Points also notified the women that they would be receiving the Pennsylvania State Police Outstanding Citizenship Award on July 30, 2003, in Hershey, Pennsylvania.

"There were some people who are alive probably because of them. Others were comforted by them because they were there; they made a terrible situation a whole lot better," he said at the ceremony. After the ceremony, Points asked to speak privately to the women, and what he said, they would never forget. "These young ladies were called angels, and I thought at first that might be a stretch. But these young ladies were running in to save others while others were running out to save themselves," said Points.

The women's story quickly gained national attention. During the summer of 2003, six of the IUP Women Rugby players posed for pictures wearing their uniforms and holding a rugby ball in Jamie Noble's car. They were being photographed for *Reader's Digest's* "Everyday Hero" section, which is dedicated to ordinary citizens who commit brave acts to help someone else. Their stories, along with the photographs, were published during the fall of 2003.

Shortly after, *Reader's Digest* challenged its audience to help select a Hero of the Year for 2003. The magazine announced that they had "profiled twelve of the most extraordinary Americans we know" and were accepting votes online for Hero of the Year. The women's story was published again with the contest.

Naturally competitive, the women began calling and e-mailing family and friends to encourage them to vote for the team. They received thousands of votes and were notified in March of 2004 that they had won Heroes of the Year for 2003.

"Being featured in *Reader's Digest* was very humbling," said Molly. "At the same time, it was surreal. People would tell you that they saw you in the magazine, and you wondered if it was all really happening."

To honor the heroes, *Reader's Digest* invited the women

to ring the closing bell at the New York Stock Exchange with the magazine's CEO, Tom Ryder. They were treated to an all-expenses-paid, one-night stay in New York City. They also had dinner with the magazine's representatives, attended a lunch awards ceremony, and took a tour of the NYSE. They received attention from the media when images of them ringing the closing bell were played on national news stations. Unfortunately, due to budget restrictions, only four members of the team were able to travel to New York City: Molly, who had been elected club president after Brenning; captains Chrissy May and Amanda Cobb; and former captain and president Crystal Brenning.

Being recognized by *Reader's Digest* also had monetary rewards for the club. Acting on the advice of their advisor, Molly prepared a proposal prior to the trip to help solicit donations. While in New York City, she boldly passed it to CEO Tom Ryder. Less than two weeks later, the club received a fifteen-thousand-dollar check from Reader's Digest Association Inc. for their foundation's account.

According to Molly, the proposal wouldn't have happened without the support of Dr. Joseph. He continued to support the players and offer advice to help the club move forward in a positive manner. He worked closely with Molly and other board members to help the club develop more depth and structure.

The members of the IUP Women's Rugby Club are heroes in the eyes of their community and of readers across the nation. Their story became one that families share at the dinner table and it clearly measures the progress female athletes have made in the United States. The seventeen brave women who risked their lives to save others were truly earth angels. Amazingly enough, the women who bravely stormed the turnpike on a foggy morning, not knowing what lay ahead, still saw themselves as normal college students who were in the right place at the right time. They feel they did what any other person would do—they helped. To them, it wasn't a decision to help. It was just what they did.

Rachel Stern described it as hitting the ground running. She said that the decision to help wasn't one the women pondered. They began to move quickly because there was no panic among them when they each approached their first victims. "We never stopped and wondered if we should do this," said Stern. "That is the rugby way. You think after you have already done something."

Jamie Noble's feelings regarding the women's reactions were similar. Noble thought that any other team would have done the same thing had they been in their position. However, it is impossible to speculate what anyone else's reaction would have been.

Molly still hopes that what the women did was something that everyone would do.

# Chapter Seven
## Fifteen-as-One

The game of rugby is often described as organized chaos. Its flow is similar to soccer in the sense that it is a moving game with very little stoppage. However, it is also similar to football in the sense that players are constantly making tackles. Each player is strategically placed and has a role on the pitch, whether it is strictly to distribute the ball or hook the ball in a scrum down. The combination of the constant movement and tackling make a rugby match look unorganized and messy. But rugby is anything but chaos.

Prior to beginning a match, the IUP Men's Rugby Club, the Tooters, would say a cheer. "Fifteen as one, fifteen as one, fifteen as one!" they would scream as they linked arms around each other's shoulders and bounced in a circle together. Their cheer is a representation of the game itself and the idea that each player has a unique job on the pitch. If each player does his or her job and the team performs as one organized unit, the outcome will be success and victory.

There is no doubt that the seventeen women extensively honored for their bravery and selflessness achieved victory that day. It was clear from witnesses, including police and medical personnel that they went beyond the call of duty by risking their own lives to save others. They acted quickly, confidently, and strategically to save lives. Mirroring their performance on the rugby pitch, the women immediately worked as a team. Their unique bond, familiarity with each other, and accessibility allowed them to help each other and those around them.

Molly quickly recognized how the women were naturally functioning as a team. "If someone was uneasy while helping, someone else was able to step in and help them out," said Molly. "A lot of it was about nonverbal communication and reading each other's emotions and signs. It was also about reading each other's faces."

Molly felt the trust she had built with her teammates over the course of her rugby career played a large role in their actions. She was one of many who were members of a close-knit, unique group. The unity that existed and the strength of the bond it created between teammates helped to carry them through the worst of the accident.

"We were not only teammates but also close friends. We trust that our teammates have our back on the rugby field, and we trusted that they had our back that day," said an emotional Jamie Noble.

Joeylyn Miller also recognized the strength and unity of her teammates. "We were bonded together from practice and being together all of the time. It was like you saw one person doing something and you thought, *That's my sister out there*," said Miller. "You had to do what you could to help them." Miller added that the team had a history of being social and wanting to help other people. She believes that it was in their nature to want to help.

As teammates, the women were used to working together to achieve victory. They relied on each other to make tackles, pass the ball, and score. They relied on their hooker to win the ball during a scrum down, their scrum half to distribute the ball, and their wings to sprint with the ball down the field. Many of the women were veterans who had been relying on their teammates for years. As a result, they had developed a team mind-set. Hours of playing together on the pitch had taught them about each other's strengths and weaknesses and how to read each other's expressions.

Jenna Sloan distinctly remembered how the team's rugby skills were used effectively to help them save lives. "Rugby is an intense sport that requires quick decision making and the use of verbal and nonverbal communication. When you play rugby, you have to evaluate scenarios quickly. We have to quickly communicate with each other on the pitch, and we were forced to quickly communicate with each other at the crash site."

The familiar methods of communication and functioning as one unit allowed the women to fall into a natural hierarchy. "It was easier because old patterns of communication quickly came about," said Sloan. "I think that really helped us."

The natural leaders on the field were also the natural leaders at the crash site. Steph DeHaven recalled how captains Chrissy May and Amanda Cobb took charge. "I looked up to people like Chrissy and Amanda. You saw them take charge on the field and during the accident," said DeHaven. "From my point of view, these were some of my best friends and to see them so selfless was astonishing."

DeHaven added that the team quickly followed their captains' leads, just as they would naturally do on the pitch. Before they realized it, all of the women were involved.

"We communicated back and forth. We were asking each other what anyone needed, and we would move around to help each other," DeHaven added.

The women were also in the right place at the right time. If anyone could make a difference, it was them. They were a team, and naturally, there were more of them.

"When you are a team and you are there together, it's a different environment," said Chrissy May.

"At one point, we were up in the woods, and I remember looking around and seeing my teammates with a lot of different people," she said. "We were definitely supporting each other."

May told the story of the ambulance crew members, who were emotionally exhausted from reliving the accident, laughing at one of her teammates who was trying to find a use for a medical instrument designed for a baby. According to May, the women were attempting to find uses for everything in their medical kits.

"They looked over at the girl and started laughing because we were trying to help but we didn't know all of the stuff that was in our medical equipment," said May. "They said that there was nothing that they could use that for here."

It was moments like those that made the women realize how fortunate they were to be able to help make a difference. For many of them, the question of how many more people would have died had they not intervened lingered for a long time. They also wondered how many more lives would have been saved if the drivers who were locking their car doors had helped, too, as the women ran past them into the fog and fire. No one will ever be able to answer these questions, but one point is true: the women did the best they could under the circumstances they were dealt.

*   *   *

The IUP Women's Rugby Club made history in many ways on April 5, 2003. They were credited with saving countless lives while putting themselves in direct danger. The leadership they displayed and the help they offered can easily be linked to the women's rights movement and all it has championed for.

Female athletes continue to knock down long-standing barriers associated with women's sports, and the IUP Women's Rugby Club contributed to this. They helped to put a spotlight on women's rugby, one of the fastest growing sports in the nation, while also displaying the excellent qualities that surface from being part of a team.

A short time ago, women who were interested in or participated in sports were labeled tomboys because it was believed that sports were only for men. Women were teased, insulted, and made to feel inferior. Footballs and baseballs were hidden and replaced with dolls and princesses. However, women's sports have advanced far enough that the stereotype seems to be disappearing, opening more doors for female athletes. In addition to rugby, women now play soccer and football, and they wrestle. These are all sports that at one point were deemed only for men.

The IUP Women's Rugby Club's actions emphasize the social evolution of female athletes and the empowerment they feel and strength they receive from playing team sports. It is an ongoing battle, but with help from pioneers, such as female CEOs, entrepreneurs, and political candidates, and laws like Title IX, progress will continue.

Julie Foudy, an eighteen-year member of the United States Women's National Soccer team, Olympic gold medalist, and advocate for women's rights, understands the impact playing sports and being a part of a team has on women.

"There are more than physical positives to playing sports," said Foudy. "All of the benefits that women gain from sports are very powerful tools for life, such as the confidence to step into a situation like the one the IUP Women's Rugby Club experienced and know they can make a difference. It also gives women the confidence to trust teammates and to understand the most effective means to operate, to understand leadership roles, and to understand how group dynamics work."

Foudy added that women playing sports also learn how to deal with pressure situations and how to be effective without panicking.

Foudy believes this social evolution will only progress in a positive manner and is a direct impact of Title IX. According to Foudy, when Title IX was enacted in 1972, one in twenty-seven women played sports. Now one in three, or even more, plays sports.

"You are going to see more women running Fortune 500 companies or being entrepreneurs, and we are already seeing the numbers of female enrollees increase at medical and law schools," said Foudy. "Women's sports in the United States will continue to excel because we have had such progressive movements toward women's athletics. I don't think it is too far-fetched to say that it is a direct product of Title IX."

# Chapter Eight
## A Surprise That Never Was

When Kim Atkins received a telephone call around eleven o'clock on the morning of Saturday, April 5, 2003, from her older sister Anna Coventry, she thought it would provide an exciting update on their youngest sister's trip home. Olivia and her family were due to arrive in Connecticut in a few hours, and the entire family was happily anticipating their long-awaited arrival. But the conversation was not one of joy and excitement.

After talking to Anna, Kim realized that she needed to get to her father. After all, at Olivia's wish, her pending month-long visit was a surprise for him. Now Kim and her family were faced with two problems. First, they would have to tell their father, Joseph, that Olivia was planning on surprising him with a visit. But after the phone call, they didn't know if she was ever going to visit again.

"My sister Anna called to tell me that she received a call from David's father, Ethan. She said Ethan was acting different and frantic and she couldn't understand him," said Kim.

Through his high emotion and tears, Ethan told Anna that the kids, David, and Olivia, had been in an accident. Moments before, he had received a call from David who had informed him that the accident had happened on the Pennsylvania Turnpike. David kept repeating, "Olivia and the kids are dead, Dad." Unfortunately, this information would be the only information either family would have for hours—with no proof it was accurate.

Thinking they might be able to reach someone, both sisters called Olivia's and David's phones, but they began to lose hope as no one answered. Frantic and scared, the women devised a plan to break the news to their father, who was still unaware of Olivia's surprise visit.

After much deliberation, the women decided that they should be together when they told their father. Kim quickly called her dad and asked him to meet her at Anna's house. When he arrived, he got out of his car and immediately noticed that Kim had been crying. When he asked if everything was okay, Kim said no and that they had some bad news. They went inside Anna's house, and he quickly noticed that Anna had also been crying. Knowing Anna was pregnant, Joseph asked if everything was okay with his unborn grandchild.

The conversation that occurred next was one that families just shouldn't have to have.

"We told him that Olivia, David, and the kids were on their way here," said Kim. "He got very excited, but then we told him about Ethan's call to Anna."

Joseph immediately became worried and wanted more information. Trying to remain optimistic, the family began notifying other family members. They called Olivia's brother in Texas and their aunts Caroline and Morrine, who were also trying to get information. They spent the next few hours calling the Pennsylvania State Police and hospitals. Not knowing the status of their family members was gut-wrenching and horrifying. Still, the families called every five to ten minutes.

After several hours of describing their missing loved ones to various hospitals and agencies, the family finally got a break.

"Anna called the hospital again around 3:00 PM and spoke with a nurse who was very helpful. I think she felt our pain and said she would do anything she could to get us an answer," said Kim.

The nurse called the family back two hours later and sadly informed them that there had been three fatalities, a woman and two children.

"We knew in our hearts that it was them," said Kim. "They didn't have names or identification on them, but we knew."

Like everyone in the family, Olivia's father was heartbroken by the loss of his youngest child. When the day began, he had been a father and grandfather who was hours from being surprised with a visit from his daughter and her family. Losing his own wife only five years earlier to cancer made him even more vulnerable.

"At the exact moment the nurse told us about the fatalities, Dad finally lost it," said Kim. "I remember vividly that he just hit his fist on the table three times and screamed, 'No, no, no!'"

It didn't take long for the family to realize that Joseph might need some medication to calm him down. Soon after, Kim and her husband took Joseph to meet his doctor.

While they were gone, a Connecticut state trooper came to Anna's house with the horrible news that Olivia, Isabella, and Noah had perished.

$$* \quad * \quad *$$

David Moyer had done everything he could to save his family. As Kim and her family would soon learn, he nearly died himself trying to get his family out of the burning car.

Olivia was less fortunate. She couldn't get her seat belt off.

"I can just picture her being nervous. The kids are in the back, there is smoke and fire, and I can just see her getting really nervous," said Kim. "She couldn't undo her seat belt.

The smoke and fire were too much. I think it just happened so fast."

It is impossible to imagine how the four of them must have felt—the father unable to save his family, the mother unable to save her children or herself, and the children, one too young to know how to unhook his car seat and one probably too terrified to even consider undoing her seat belt.

After David was pulled away from the burning car, he called his father.

*       *       *

It is impossible to comprehend how a visit that was supposed to be filled with laughter, memories, and love ended so terribly and quickly. It was a week before David returned to his father's house in Connecticut. He also traveled to Pennsylvania with his brother to claim the remains of his family.

The funeral was held on Saturday, April 12. The funeral parlor was lined with flowers, as friends and families spent hours remembering the ones they loved. Isabella's school and Girl Scout troop sent flowers, and a number of friends and David's superiors flew to Connecticut to pay their respects. Friends of the Moyers from Saint Francis army base also set up a scholarship fund in the Moyer family's name.

Ironically, the funeral fell on the same day that Anna's baby shower was originally planned to be held. Because the hall was already reserved and the food ordered for the shower, the families decided to use the location for the after-funeral luncheon. They quickly informed the hall that there would be more people attending and that the event had changed.

The army granted David a leave of absence. They packed up the family's belongings and shipped them to David in Connecticut.

According to Kim, the first thing he said when he came home was he was sorry. He felt so much guilt because he couldn't save his family.

"David kept saying, 'If we would have done this differently …' He kept blaming himself every step of the way," said Kim. "He felt as though it was his fault."

*     *     *

Kim Atkins remembers her sister Olivia as the happy and loving person she was. She considers herself lucky that she had the chance to experience and understand the kind of love they shared. She believes that Olivia and her children became angels on that foggy morning. Her words during one of our first e-mails put it all in perspective, describing how she dealt with three horrific losses.

"The only blessing that day is that they all went together. My sister would not have been able to live without her children nor them without her," she wrote. "I finally learned to have faith that some things are just meant to be."

Kim also believes that the IUP Women's Rugby Club

members are truly angels. In the same e-mail, she wrote, "We think that they are the most caring and compassionate individuals, who, as we now know, have made such a difference that day in so many ways. They were the light that so many people needed. We believe that they are true living angels on the earth."

Not a day goes by that Kim doesn't think of her sister, niece, and nephew. She still feels them with her every day and is intent on their memory living on. This is clearly displayed in the Web site that she created with her husband and daughters in their memory. The pictures and poems are enough to make even the most stoic of viewers tear up.

Olivia's family also finds comfort in the little things that almost seem like they were meant to be, such as that Olivia's handwritten recipes that David later delivered to her sisters and the pictures of the kids that Olivia intended to distribute during their visit were miraculously untouched when the car burned. Anna named her daughter, born two months after the accident, Sophia Olivia, after the grandmother and aunt that she would never meet.

# Chapter Nine
# More Than a Team

Lauren Culley doesn't take her shoes off during long car rides anymore. After witnessing accident victims hopping out of their cars and running to safety shoeless, Culley is afraid to be left barefoot. She is also apprehensive while driving next to tractor trailers, and for weeks after the accident, she suffered from nightmares.

Rachel Stern became afraid of the dark and slept with her light on. She, too, suffered from intense nightmares.

Steph DeHaven used to enjoy watching the movie *Final Destination 2*, which includes graphic scenes that portray horrible, multiple-vehicle crashes. The scenes are so similar to what she witnessed on the turnpike that DeHaven can't watch the movie anymore. It is simply too emotional for her.

For weeks after the accident, every time she went to bed,

Ariel Baum pictured the accident scene. The smoke-filled sky and images of people suffering and crying for help were too much for her to bear.

To the group of young college students, it seems as if their lives were split into two time frames. There was life before the accident and life after the accident. Life after the accident began as soon as the women finally closed the doors to their cars to leave the scene. The reality of what they experienced took some time to sink in as they drove away in complete silence.

Rachel Stern remembers leaving the accident scene and wondering if it was a nightmare. Afraid and emotional, Stern began shaking terribly, which lasted the entire ride back to IUP.

After a team discussion, some of the women continued with their trip to Shippensburg to meet the rest of the team and play their match. Although they were exhausted from hours of providing first aid and their emotions were running high, the women were in need of a distraction. They took to the pitch but were unable to defeat Shippensburg.

According to Stephanie DeHaven, who uncharacteristically only played half of the match, there were a lot of passes being dropped and the team wasn't clicking. The fast-paced, highly competitive team was playing as if they had no connection to each other and were unable to bring everything together as a team.

Regardless, they earned respect from their opponents

for taking the field after everything they had witnessed that morning.

Passing the crash site on their way home the next day was also extremely difficult for the women who had traveled to Shippensburg. With the prior day's events replaying freshly in their minds, they were filled with sadness and disbelief. The road was still scorched from multiple vehicle fires, and damaged guardrails lined the turnpike.

The rest of the team returned immediately to IUP, unable to bear the thought of playing rugby after being subjected to such sorrow and grief. They gathered at the rugby house, where they spent most of the night talking and comforting each other. For the majority of them, they were able to find the most comfort at the rugby house, in the company of their teammates. The nights of talking and sharing continued throughout the spring semester as the women grew even closer. Some nights, they played their own version of foursquare into the wee hours of the morning, and other nights, they watched movies together. Sometimes it didn't matter what they were doing; they just wanted the sense of security that they felt from being together.

Ariel Baum described the Saturday night of the accident and the nights that followed as abnormal. Most Saturday nights after a match, the women would socialize and celebrate. However, the unfortunate circumstances of the day carried over into the evening, and they felt no need to celebrate or socialize. Their young lives had been altered, and some of their youth had been stolen from them.

Jamie Noble benefited tremendously from the additional time spent with teammates. After individually attending one university-sponsored counseling session, Noble realized that being with her teammates and talking about what happened was more beneficial.

Noble was not alone; many of the women continued to struggle with outsiders who couldn't understand the impact the accident was having on their lives. They experienced a loss of innocence and then a separation from the rest of the university's student population. They had seen bodies charred by smoke and fire, still lying in the cars that became their graves. They had seen young children caked in blood and disoriented parents who were trying to care for them. They had seen families separated and panicked, trying to find their loved ones. They had seen paramedics, firefighters, police officers, and medics trying to take control of what felt like an out-of-control situation. They had seen more death and destruction that day on the mountain than many people witness in a lifetime. Although their family and friends continuously offered support and compassion, the women leaned and depended on each other.

As Rachel Stern put it, they went from being children to adults in one day. "We were kids that believed in Santa that morning, but by the end of the day, an adult shook us and said Santa didn't exist." Even though she had grown up in a close-knit family where she never left the house without telling her parents that she loved them, Stern shared no accident details with her parents. She only wanted to talk to her teammates. Although other team members who weren't there were sympathetic, sharing stories still wasn't the same. No one who wasn't there could really comprehend it. To this day, Stern still struggles with April 5 every year. She breaks down and gives thanks for adding another year to her life. It is a special day for her—one that she believes has made her the person she is today.

Difficulty also arose as the women continued to receive recognition for their selfless actions. Although they were grateful for the numerous events the university held in their honor, it also made it difficult because they had to relive the experience each time they were recognized. The feelings of guilt for not being able to save everyone were enough to make their stomachs ache as they bravely put on smiles and responded gratefully for the recognition. At the same time, some of the women felt that the recognition wasn't necessary. They felt they were the only natural choice to help, because they were a team and there were more of them. The women wondered why they were being recognized when they did what every decent human should do.

More questions arose as the pieces of the day were put together. A lot of the women believe that fate played a large role in what happened. They spent time talking about timing and how they barely missed being directly involved in the accident. If they hadn't stopped to use the bathroom prior to getting onto the turnpike, would their cars have been struck? There was also the possibility that fate delayed them to allow them to help accident victims instead of missing the accident completely.

A few months after the accident, the women received a letter from a man who wrote that he had been in the gas station parking lot at the time the women were there. He wrote that he couldn't get out because the women were blocking the entrance and exit. He was intending to drive eastbound on the turnpike, and the caravan was delaying his trip. Shortly after, he received a call on his phone telling him not to get on the turnpike. Had the women not blocked his way, he may have gotten onto the turnpike and may have been involved in the accident.

It was a twist of fate for the women also. Molly had forgotten her wallet, and the entire caravan had waited for her. Everyone wondered but will never know if the delay saved their lives. If they had gotten on the turnpike minutes earlier, they could have been in the tragic accident.

Fate also played a role in bringing together seventeen of the most compassionate, selfless, and fearless college women. It wasn't by chance that these seventeen women were traveling together that morning. But it was by choice that they left their safe cars to help the helpless. When other people were locking their doors, the women were opening their own. It was by choice that they comforted victims and applied pressure to wounds. It was by choice that they moved debris off the turnpike and spent hours helping emergency services filter through everything.

Perhaps the only positive thing that came from this disastrous event was that the accident made the women realize they were more than a team. They grew closer as they shared their experiences with each other. They became sisters in every sense of the word. Working together side by side for hours helped them bond. No other experience in their lives, before or after, has had such an effect.

# Chapter Ten
## Mile Marker 166

Joseph Brimmeier drives past mile marker 166 on the Pennsylvania Turnpike twice a week on his way to and from Harrisburg. Not once has he made the trip without thinking about what he considers one of the worst accidents in the turnpike's sixty-nine-year history.

A native of Pittsburgh, Brimmeier had served only a short eight weeks in his newly appointed position of chief executive officer of the Pennsylvania Turnpike Commission when the April 5, 2003, fog-related accident occurred. Having never worked at an agency like the turnpike commission that must handle tragic accidents, Brimmeier was overwhelmingly affected. The tragic and unnecessary injuries and loss of life had such a profound impact on Brimmeier that he knew the turnpike commission had to react to prevent similar accidents from occurring. The Pennsylvania Turnpike already was considered a very safe interstate, with one of the lowest fatality rates in the nation. Most incidents that did occur were isolated. What happened on April 5, 2003, was a rarity, especially because multiple lives were lost. With that to consider, Brimmeier knew he needed to make the turnpike even safer and he needed to do it quickly.

Although the turnpike commission was already abiding by the normal federal highway guidelines on that stretch of the road by posting large diamond-shaped fog warning signs throughout the mountainous area, which Brimmeier knew was prone to fog and blizzards, he began to look into additional options immediately. He knew he couldn't fix the hazardous weather conditions that plagued that portion of the road, but he felt he needed to minimize the possibility of an accident this tragic happening again.

"To have an accident of that magnitude happen to me while I am sitting in that chair over there, two months after I get here, and having it be one of the worst accidents we have ever had on the turnpike and to have the loss of lives that happened that day, I mean, you would have to be an emotionless person if it didn't have a huge impact on you," said Brimmeier. Speaking in a genuine tone, Brimmeier added that he thought about the accident a lot, and after recreating the accident scene, he declared that the turnpike commission had to find a way to make that stretch of highway safer. He knew he wanted a fog-detection system and quickly met with representatives from transportation engineering firm

Orth-Rodgers & Associates Inc. Their goal was to design and build a system that would save lives and prevent unnecessary accidents in a dangerous stretch of the turnpike.

On November 14, 2005, the Pennsylvania Turnpike Commission held a press conference at mile marker 166 to unveil their $5.7 million fog-detection and traveler-alert network. The Fog Detection, Traveler Information, and Dynamic Traffic Control System, also referred to as the "fog-warning system," is designed to warn approaching motorists of unsafe conditions along the ten-mile stretch of mountainous, fog-prone turnpike where the accident occurred. It covers the area from mile marker 171.6 to 162.1, between the Breezewood interchange and the Sideling Hill service plaza.

"It's a total weather detection system," said Brimmeier. "Once it's activated, everything goes into place. The speed limits are reduced based on visibility, the state police increase patrolling in the area, and tractor trailers and buses are required to move into the right lane."

The network is composed of nine remote traffic monitoring systems (RTMS) and nine roadway weather information stations (RWIS), which are located on the shoulders of the eastbound and westbound lanes of the ten-mile stretch. The RTMSs monitor motorists' speed through the area by collecting vehicle data. The RWISs house static cameras and collect weather-related information, such as roadway temperature, wind speed, visibility, sight distance, and barometric pressure.

The RWISs are placed about one mile apart and check visibility readings for that stretch of the road every thirty seconds. If necessary, based on these readings, they activate. If the weather conditions are dangerous, the system will react by categorizing them into one of three thresholds. Threshold one occurs when the system determines that visibility on the mountain has dropped below one-half mile. At this point, the speed limit is automatically reduced from sixty-five miles per hour to fifty miles per hour. Threshold two occurs when visibility drops to five hundred feet, and the speed limit is automatically reduced to forty miles per hour. Threshold three occurs when visibility drops to 325 feet. Again, speed limits are impacted as the limit is automatically reduced to thirty miles per hour.

The necessary safety precautions are also communicated to traveling motorists by way of road signs. The ten-mile stretch has ten dynamic message signs (DMS). Nine of the message signs are designed to display three messages regarding weather-related warnings. The first message reads, "Reduced Vision Ahead"; the second message also informs motorists that the speed is reduced ahead; and the third message reads, "Trucks Keep Right." The tenth sign is used to report any incidents at the Breezewood interchange.

There are also other dynamics of the system that are used to communicate weather-related problems. An additional twenty-five changeable speed limit signs exist along the stretch to post suitable speeds. Numerous cameras are also used to help determine visibility from the operations center, which is located in Harrisburg and monitors the system twenty-four hours a day. Surface sensors are also used to determine the temperature of the roadway. In blizzard-like conditions, this helps the commission's maintenance department determine when salt needs to be spread. Additionally, the Pennsylvania State Police are notified and patrol the ten-mile stretch more frequently as hazardous weather conditions arise.

"We are doing everything we can to prevent another accident from occurring in that stretch of the turnpike," said Brimmeier. "We believe we have a good system; however, nothing is fail-safe."

Although the turnpike commission reports they have had fewer fog-related incidents since the fog-detection system was installed, they can't confirm if that is a direct result of the system or if the fog hasn't been as severe as it was on April 5, 2003. They do recognize that it is the vehicle operator's responsibility to respond to the system's communications.

"The system is designed and created to communicate a condition to our customers. The customer has to react," said Carl DeFebo Jr., media and public relations manager for the Pennsylvania Turnpike Commission. DeFebo added that customers need to be paying attention to the messages being communicated to them.

In addition to being recognized as a necessary, potentially

lifesaving network by the turnpike commission, the fog-warning system was also highly regarded by the transportation and engineering community.

In May 2006 the fog-detection system received an award for its deployment and activation. The Intelligent Transportation Society of America (ITS-America), a not-for-profit organization that focuses on fostering the use of advanced technologies in surface transportation systems, named it the ITS-America Best New Product, Service, or Application.

Shortly thereafter, the turnpike commission received notification that the project had won an award from the Federal Highway Administration (FHWA) in the category of 2006 excellence in highway design. A few weeks later, Orth-Rodgers & Associates Inc. was notified that they, along with the turnpike commission, were again going to be recognized for the project. This time, it was by the American Council of Engineering Companies of Pennsylvania (ACEC/PA), who awarded both organizations the 2007 Diamond Honor Award for the fog-detection system.

The engineering excellence awards (EEA) are focused on honoring the industry's best projects for the year as submitted by the ACEC members. The prestigious awards are organized by ACEC, who select a judging panel to determine the top twenty-four winners. Because the project had won an award from ACEC/PA, Orth-Rodgers was invited to participate in the ACEC 2007 EEA. As suggested, they submitted the project. In February 2007 Orth-Rodgers & Associates Inc. was notified by ACEC that the fog-warning system had achieved national finalist status in the 2007 EEA competition.

The Pennsylvania Turnpike Commission can't alter the tragic events that occurred on April 5, 2003. They can't change the fact that four people died or that many, many more were seriously injured. They know that many lives were altered forever and that a group of young college rugby players witnessed death and destruction. But what they could change, they did.

The commission took what they knew, which was that the stretch of road on which the April 5 tragedies occurred was prone to hazardous driving conditions, and they made that section of the road safer. Acting cautiously and with the intent of preventing future accidents from occurring, the commission installed their fog-detection system and created a stretch of highway that would protect their customers. Understanding completely that they couldn't alter the weather conditions, the commission instead chose to alter the highway to accommodate the hazardous conditions that could occur. In doing so, they made an already safe interstate that is traveled by millions of drivers every year even safer.

# Chapter Eleven
## Earth Angels

Nine months after the accident, Molly's father responded to an e-mail she sent him. He wrote, "With all the references to angels in the past nine months, I am starting to believe that maybe you all truly are angels." As the events that occurred continued to emerge, it was hard not to believe the women really were angels on earth, especially when first reading the e-mail Molly sent her father.

The original e-mail was sent to Molly from Olivia's aunt Caroline. A family member had showed Caroline the *Reader's Digest* that published the women's story, and Caroline found them through correspondence with the university.

In her e-mail, a compassionate, grateful Caroline shared a lot of intimate details about her family, including how they coped with the traumatic loss of their loved ones. She also talked about traveling to the spot of the accident to say good-bye to Olivia and the children. Caroline had even been in touch with Olivia's best friend and neighbor, who shared with Caroline a description of how the house looked; she said it was waiting for the Moyers to return. According to the neighbor, Isabella's school photos were still on the table and toys were scattered where Noah had been playing.

However, looking past her sorrow and grief, Caroline also made a reference to angels. "This terrible tragedy has a silver lining of sorts and that is because my life has once again been touched by angels," she wrote. "We will never forget your heroic efforts, and all of us appreciate and love you for being there and helping. We consider you *our* angels now."

Molly was grateful for the e-mail. "After the accident, we wanted any information on any of the people that we talked to, that we tried to comfort. We wanted to know that they were okay, but that information was not available to us." When Caroline found the women, Molly claimed it did help her heal. It was also difficult because Caroline was reaching out to the girls and was kind and thankful for their heroic actions. Yet Caroline was the one person who had contacted them about family members who didn't survive. Additionally, with every correspondence and all the details learned, Molly painfully relived the accident.

"We weren't able to help her family, and she was reaching out and saying all of these nice things," said Molly.

The relationship between Caroline and Molly, as well as a few of the other team members, lasted for months. Caroline frequently telephoned the women's rugby house, where Molly lived, and talked to the women. She e-mailed pictures of her family, invited the women to visit her, and even sent Molly a beautiful bracelet for her twenty-first birthday. Caroline's thoughts were also included in the book of quotes given to Molly by her parents when she turned twenty-one, a book that even today she holds dear to her. The relationship the women formed is evidence that Molly is a strong, compassionate woman who helped ease the pain of others.

Tremendously moved by Caroline, Molly used pictures of Olivia, Isabella, and Noah and completed an art project for her Print Making II class. She drew the back of a person with wings and a halo and placed superimposed pictures of Olivia, Isabella, and Noah on the wings, mixed in with the color black. The idea came from Caroline, who often called the women "earth angels." The project served as a form of therapy and an outlet for Molly, because it allowed her to express and expose her feelings. It also brought to life the loving, caring mother and her two children that Molly had learned so much about after their deaths. And for Molly, it helped give them a face. After receiving recognition for something that she didn't consider a choice but instead a natural instinct, Molly felt like she was giving back.

"I solidified a connection with Caroline by sharing pictures and stories," said Molly. "The project was extremely beneficial because I wasn't hiding or avoiding my feelings while working on it."

Although this was one of the positive outcomes of the accident, there were also many negatives. Sometimes the negative implications and indications of the severity of what she had survived appeared when Molly least expected them. For almost a year after the accident, Molly couldn't ride in a car when she was not driving. She was afraid to not be in control.

Molly distinctly remembers moving Sarah out of her college apartment at Shippensburg University. Her parents and Sarah's boyfriend were in two different cars, and Molly and Sarah were driving together on the Pennsylvania Turnpike. Sarah was driving, and Molly suddenly felt like April 5, 2003, was going to happen again. As she continued to replay the accident scene in her mind, Molly was visualizing her family members involved in an accident.

"I had a complete panic attack and forced my sister to pull the car over. I was crying hysterically but felt really silly that I was feeling that way."

Eventually, Sarah asked if Molly wanted to drive. But after a highly charged panic attack, Molly felt she wasn't able to.

Even when she was busy living the life of an easygoing, average college student, the tragedies that Molly had witnessed managed to creep into her daily life.

A few months after the accident, Molly and Chrissy May were in a video rental store picking a movie. Molly picked up *Ghost Ship*. On the front of the DVD case was a

3-D picture of a face that changed images when moved in different directions. When the face switched from a nice, normal face to a rotten, decomposed one, it was simply too much for Molly to bear. The resemblance to the charred bodies Molly had seen was too great.

"There are repercussions like that where you don't think they are going to affect you. I threw the DVD because it looked like what I saw. Your everyday stuff like that affects you because you were there."

Saturday, April 5, 2003, began like any other rugby Saturday for Molly and her sixteen teammates. However, it ended in a way that none of them could have ever imagined. In just a few hours, they fought for their own lives while fighting for the lives of strangers that they would never meet again. They helped stop bleeding wounds, moved injured victims away from burning vehicles, and reconnected families. They administered multiple forms of first aid and comforted dozens of victims without any regard for themselves.

Like all of the women who were by her side, Molly has never forgotten what she witnessed and the lives she helped to save. The images of death and the fear she felt are forever etched in her mind. The bond she created with her teammates continues to exist, regardless of the months or years that fall between contacts. She remembers them as the confident, selfless women who saved countless lives on that foggy April morning; even more, she remembers them as the angels they are.